To a fine "new" brother, Shawn, who in a
few years will be able to read to
his "new" brother, Ryan. With

The Nelsons, the Marstadts, and
the Leiktiegs, June 21, 1981

Aesop's Fables

AESOP'S FABLES

with illustrations by
Percy J. Billinghurst
in color by
Martina Selway

CASTLE
BOOKS

AESOP'S FABLES

Text: The 75 fables for this book have been
newly written, from traditional sources, by
HAZEL SHERTZER

Illustrations: The illustrations for this book have
been adapted and colored by
MARTINA SELWAY,
from original black-and-white drawings by
PERCY J. BILLINGHURST
first published in 1899

LOC No: 80-65342
ISBN No: 0-89009-350-4

Manufactured in the United States of America

Contents

THE·COCK AND THE·FOX.

1. The Cock and the Fox

A fox set up his home near a hen-roost in order to more easily attack the chickens. A cock saw him and immediately started to run away as fast as he could, and the other birds laughed at him. "Listen," he said, pausing, "only the other day a fox caught hold of me and I was very fortunate to get away. Tell me, if any of you had been in my position would you also not be scared of even the fox's foot-print, let alone the sight of him?"

Moral: Once bitten, twice shy.

2. The Peacock

The peacock used to be distinguished only by a crest of feathers on his head, but one day he asked Jupiter if he might not also be given a train. The peacock was rather a favourite and so his wish was granted and he was given a most magnificent train of feathers, the envy of all the other birds. Since this change in his appearance, the peacock assumed many airs and graces and strutted about the farmyard with great dignity, to the amazement of the other farmyard birds. However, when the peacock tried to fly he could not, because of his heavy train. He realized that he had sacrificed this ability and was now hampered by the glory of his own feathers.

Moral: Do not sacrifice your basic activities just for the sake of your looks.

3. The Cuckoo, the Hedge-sparrow and the Owl

A lazy cuckoo who could not be bothered to make a home for herself, laid her eggs in a nest built by a hedge-sparrow, who hatched them and brought them up herself until they were able to fly away and look after themselves. The cuckoo then complained to an owl that the hedge-sparrow had ignored her, in spite of the confidence the cuckoo had shown in her for allowing her to care for her young. "And as for my young ones," continued the cuckoo, "they have flown off without a single word of thanks to me, when I am their natural mother after all." "Be quiet," said the owl, "it is you who should thank the hedge-sparrow for taking care of your brood, and why should they be grateful to you anyway when you abandoned them?"

Moral: Before expecting gratitude from others, you should learn to be grateful yourself.

4. The Dog and the Shadow

As a dog was crossing a river with a large piece of meat in his mouth, he thought he saw another dog under the water also holding some meat. He did not realise that it was only his own reflection in the water, but out of greed he tried to snatch the meat away from the other dog and, of course, dropped his piece into the water.

Moral: If you want too much you may lose what you already have.

THE·DOG AND THE·SHADOW.

JUPITER AND THE·CAMEL·

5. Jupiter and the Camel

It very much annoyed the camel that bulls, stags, lions and bears had horns, teeth and claws while he had nothing with which to defend himself. He asked the god Jupiter to give him a pair of horns but Jupiter became angry at this request and instead of giving him horns he decided to take away his ears instead.

Moral: Be thankful for the things you have and do not always wish to have what you do not need.

6. The Diamond and the Glow-worm

A diamond fell out of a young lady's ring one evening. A glow-worm who saw it sparkling as it fell, began to mock it when the night came and it no longer shone. "Where is your brilliance now, you famous diamond? See how you cannot compete with my superior blaze," the glow-worm boasted. "You conceited insect," said the diamond, "you only owe your brilliance to the darkness which surrounds you, while I shine in the daylight and the brighter the day, the more brilliantly I sparkle, whereas the daylight shows you up to be no more than a tiny worm."

Moral: Something of true worth can be recognized in the light of day.

7. The Fox and the Sick Lion

A lion fell sick one day and stayed in his cave. He noticed that of all the animals, the fox never came to visit him. He sent a message to the fox saying how displeased he was and how he would be very glad to have a visit from him. The fox wrote back, hoping for his speedy recovery, but saying that he had noticed many animals going in to see the lion, but not one coming out again.

Moral: Beware the cunning schemes of other people.

8. The Dog in the Manger

A disagreeable nasty dog jumped into a manger and started barking and growling so that the animals could not get to their food. The dog himself did not eat the same food but still would not let the other animals near, preferring to go hungry himself rather than let anyone else eat.

Moral: Do not take something from someone else when you cannot even use it yourself.

9. The Fox and the Crab

A sharp-eyed fox saw a crab lying on the sands and carried him away to eat him. When the crab realised he was going to be eaten he said to himself, "It is my own fault for being on the sands instead of in the sea, where I belong."

Moral: You should not feel sorry for someone who finds himself in trouble due to his own foolishness.

THE·DOG·IN·THE·MANGER.

THE ✿ SHEPHERD'S ✿ BOY.

10. The Fox and the Crocodile

There was a discussion between a fox and a crocodile about their ancestors. The crocodile said many wonderful things about the family he had come from and his superior ancestry. The fox only smiled and said, "One need only look at you to see your background; you carry the marks of it in your skin."
Moral: You cannot boast about things that are plain for all to see.

11. The Cock and the Jewel

A cock who was scratching around for food found a precious jewel. He said to it, "If your owner had found you, he would be so happy, but I am not for I have no use for you. I would much rather have one barleycorn than all the jewels in the world."
Moral: Know exactly what you want in life.

12. The Shepherd's Boy

There was once a boy in charge of a flock of sheep who began to call out that there was a wolf attacking the sheep when in fact no wolf was there. He did this to make the people in the town run out to help him in the fields and when they came he laughed and said there was no wolf after all. One day a wolf did come and he cried "Wolf! Wolf!" but nobody took any notice of him and the wolf killed all the sheep.
Moral: If we tell lies no-one will believe us when we tell the truth.

13. The Fox and the Lion

A fox happened to walk in the path of a lion and as this was the first time he had seen a lion he was very frightened. Some time later he saw another lion and, although he still felt frightened, he did not fear the second lion quite so much. Later still he met another lion and this time he felt brave enough to go up to the lion and start to talk to him.

Moral: Once we are used to something, we are no longer frightened by it.

14. The Owl and the Nightingale

An old, solemn owl had lived for many years in the ruins of an old monastery and had read so many of the ancient manuscripts, that he thought he was very wise and would sit for whole days with his eyes half-shut, thinking he was deep and clever. One evening as he sat meditating and half asleep, a nightingale perched near him and began to sing very sweetly. He started awake and with a horrid screech interrupted her. "Go away," he said, "you stupid song-bird, do not distract my deep thoughts with your noise. Harmony lies in truth which is gained by study and not by your warbling notes." "You conceited bird," said the nightingale, "music is a natural expression of beauty and even if you do not appreciate it, there are many others of taste who admire and love it."

Moral: Be aware of all the natural beauty around you, before you consider yourself educated.

THE·FOX AND THE·LION

THE·FROGS·DESIRING·A·KING.

15. The Hares and the Foxes

The hares once started a war with the eagles and asked the foxes to help them. The foxes said, ''We would willingly help you if we did not know who you are and with whom you are fighting.''

Moral: Know your own limitations.

16. The Frogs Desiring a King

A long time ago when frogs lived freely in the lakes, they grew tired of living without a government and asked Jupiter for a king to rule over them. Jupiter, who knew them well, threw down a log to be their ruler. The splash the log made when it first fell frightened the frogs enough to keep them in awe of it for some time. After a while though, one bold frog went up to the log and sat on it and, of course the other frogs soon copied him and eventually they lost all respect for the log. They went again to Jupiter and said that the king he had sent them was too tame and could he supply another. So Jupiter sent a stork to be their king and the frogs were not at all happy, because the stork took away all their freedom and used to eat some of them. They then asked Mercury to go to Jupiter and ask for yet another king but this time Jupiter replied by saying ''If you are not happy when things are well, you must be patient when things go wrong.''

Moral: If you are not content with things as they are and you change them, you must not then complain if you are then even worse off.

17. The Crow and the Pitcher

A crow that was extremely thirsty found a pitcher with some water in it, but the water was right at the bottom of the pitcher and he could not reach it. At first he tried to break the jug, then over-turn it, but it was too heavy for him. At last he thought of a way to reach the water. He dropped a great many little pebbles into it until the level of the water was high enough for him to drink.

Moral: Careful thought can provide the answer to a difficult situation.

18. The Wind and the Sun

An argument once took place between the North Wind and the sun as to which was the stronger of the two. They saw a man walking along and each said that they could get his cloak off him, and it would show who was the better of the two. The North Wind began to blow very fiercely but the man only drew his cloak tighter round him, and the stronger the wind blew the more tightly the man wrapped his cloak round him. The sun then began to shine and as the man grew warm he unfastened his cloak and, as the sun shone even more brightly, the man eventually took his cloak off.

Moral: Kindness works better than force.

THE·CROW AND THE·PITCHER.

THE·SNAKE AND THE·FILE.

19. The Fox and the Frog

A frog once came out of his pond and announced his great skill in medicine. A fox, seeing the frog's pitted skin, bulging eyes and spindly legs, said, "cure your own ills before you start meddling with other people's."
Moral: Physician, heal thyself.

20. The Snake and the File

A snake crawled into an ironmonger's shop and began to lick at a metal file. She saw that the file had blood on it and the more blood she saw the more she licked at the file because she thought it was the file that was bleeding and not herself. Finally she could lick no longer and began to bite the file but, finding this useless, she eventually left it alone.
Moral: It is useless to go on worrying at something when the only thing we are hurting is ourself.

21. The Seaside Travellers

Some travellers walking near the sea, climbed a high cliff and saw out at sea what they took to be a large ship and waited to see it reach the shore. As it came closer they saw it looked more like a small boat than a large ship, and when it reached the beach they found that it was no more than a bundle of sticks tied together.
Moral: Our biggest expectations sometimes turn out to be very small in reality.

22. The Old Man and his Sons

An old man had many sons who were always quarrelling and falling out with each other. He had often pleaded with them to live together peacefully, but to no effect. One day he called them round him and, producing a bundle of sticks, told them to try and break it in half. Each son tried with all his strength but the bundle resisted all their efforts. Then, cutting the rope which tied the sticks, he told his sons to break them separately. This they managed to do very easily. "You see, my sons," he said, "the power of unity. Bound together by brotherly love, you may defy almost anything; divided, you will fall."

Moral: Unity is strength.

23. The Jackdaw and the Peacocks

A jackdaw wanted to look more handsome and so dressed up in all the brightest feathers he could find from other birds. Once he was dressed in all their beautiful and colourful feathers he strolled about showing himself off. Eventually the other birds discovered what he had done and each bird pecked off the feathers belonging to him, until the jackdaw was left stripped of all the other birds' feathers.

Moral: You cannot disguise what you really are, even if you dress in the most beautiful clothes.

THE·JACKDAW AND THE·PEACOCKS.

THE·STAG LOOKING·INTO THE·WATER·

24. The Stag Looking into the Water

As a stag was drinking at a stream he saw his reflection in the water and began to think about his appearance. He did not like the look of his thin legs and thought his large antlers much more beautiful. As he was thinking this a pack of hunting dogs came towards him. He began to run across the fields and got away from them into a wood. Unfortunately his antlers became caught in some branches and he could not free himself so eventually the dogs found him and attacked him. The last thing he thought was that if he had had more trust and faith in his legs than in his antlers he would still be free.

Moral: Know both your strongest and weakest points.

25. The Oak and the Willow Trees

A violent storm uprooted an oak tree that grew by the bank of a river and it fell into the water. The oak drifted along the river and came to rest by some willow trees. He was surprised to find them still standing and asked how they had managed to escape the fury of the storm, which had torn him up by the roots. "We bent our heads to the wind," they said "and it passed over us. You stood stiff and stubborn until you could stand no more."

Moral: It is sometimes better to bend with the wind than to try and stand up to it.

26. The Fox and the Crow

A fox saw a crow sitting in a tree with a tasty-looking piece of food in her beak. The fox very much wanted this food and tried to think of a way to get it away from the crow. He called out to her, "You beautiful bird, you look so lovely and graceful sitting high up there in the tree like some fabulous creature from another world. Can you also sing as beautifully?" The crow was so flattered by his words that she immediately opened her beak and began to sing, dropping the food down to the ground where the fox eagerly picked it up and hurried away with it.

Moral: Beware of flattery, it can make you forget what is sensible.

27. The Ant and the Dove

An ant went to the bank of a river to take a drink of water but was swept away and nearly drowned. A dove sitting in a tree overlooking the river, took a leaf and threw it into the water near the ant. The ant climbed onto it and was floated to safety. The ant hoped that one day he could repay the kindness of the dove, but he was so small and the dove was big and able to fly. Some time later a birdcatcher came, stood under the tree, and laid a trap for the dove. The ant saw him and stung his foot so that he dropped his tools, startling the dove who was able to fly away to safety.

Moral: You can always find a way to repay another's kindness.

THE·FOX AND THE·CROW.

THE·WASPS AND THE·HONEY·POT·

28. The Wasps and the Honey-pot

There was a large swarm of wasps who discovered an over-turned honey-pot. They all swooped onto it and then into it to eat the honey. But when they tried to fly away they found that they were quite stuck.

Moral: If we allow our pleasures to become too important to us we can sometimes never escape from them, even when we want to.

29. The Fox and the Stork

A fox one day invited a stork to come and have dinner with him. He played a little joke on him and put the dinner in a large, flat dish so that while he could lap it up quite easily, the stork could only dip in the tip of his long bill and could hardly eat anything. Some time later the stork invited the fox to have dinner with him. Remembering what had happened, he put some minced meat in a long, narrow-necked jar so that although he could dip in his bill and eat quite easily, the fox could hardly get at anything. The fox realised that the stork was paying him back for the trick he had played, and had to accept it.

Moral: Do not expect to play tricks on others unless you are prepared for them to do the same to you.

30. The Ape and the Dolphin

A long time ago when people went to sea they used to take with them puppies or apes to keep them amused during the journey. There was an ape on one of these journeys when the ship became ship-wrecked during a fierce storm. The men were swimming towards land and the ape was swimming with them when a dolphin, mistaking him for a man, took him upon his back and began to swim towards a place called Pyraeus. The dolphin asked the ape if he was an Athenian and the ape replied "yes, and of a very ancient family there." "Well, then", said the dolphin, "you must know Pyraeus." "Oh, very well," replied the ape, thinking it was the name of a man, "Pyraeus is a good friend of mine." When the dolphin heard this and realised how stupid the cheeky ape was, he became quite angry and let the ape fall off his back and into the sea, and was never heard of again.
Moral: Trying to impress people by boasting, lying and pretending will be found out.

31. The Bald Knight

A certain old knight, who wore a wig to hide his baldness, was out hunting one day. A sudden gust of wind carried away his wig and showed his bald head. His companions all laughed at him but the old man, instead of being upset, laughed with them. "Is it surprising," he said "that another man's hair shouldn't keep on my head when my own wouldn't stay there?"
Moral: Laugh at your troubles, and they will be lighter.

THE·APE AND THE·DOLPHIN.

THE·LARK AND ·HER YOUNG· ONES.

32. The Lark and her Young Ones

There was once a family of larks who had made their home in a cornfield. When the mother went looking for food she told the little ones to let her know any news that might happen while she was away. On her return they said that the owner of the field had been there and ordered his neighbour to reap the corn. "Well," said the mother, "there's no danger yet." The next day they told her the farmer had been again and asked his friends to reap the corn. "Well," she said, "there's still no danger." The next day she went out again and when she came back, the little ones told her the farmer had come again and he had decided to return with his son the next day and reap the corn themselves. "Now," said the mother, "it is time to look elsewhere. I had no worries about the neighbour or the friends, but the master will be as good as his word I am sure, for it is his field."

Moral: If you want a job well done, you must do it yourself and not rely on others.

33. The Fox and the Ass

An ass found a dead lion's skin, put it on, and walked about the forest. The other animals ran away in terror and he was delighted at the success of his disguise. He met a fox and rushed at him, trying to roar like a lion to frighten him even more. "Ah," said the fox, "if you had not opened your mouth, I should have been taken in like the others, but hearing you bray I know who you really are."

Moral: Your speech can give you away even if your looks do not.

34. The Wild Boar and the Fox

One day a boar was sharpening his teeth against a tree when a fox came up and asked him why he was doing that. "I can see no reason for it," said the fox. "Well, I can," said the boar, "if someone came to attack me, it would be too late to start sharpening my teeth then—I would have to fight."
Moral: It is best to be prepared for dangers, even in a time of peace.

35. The Ants and the Grasshopper

A grasshopper that had merrily sung all through the summer, was almost dying with hunger when the winter came. She went to some ants that lived near and asked them to lend her some of the food they had put by. "I will certainly repay you by next year," she said. "What did you do all the summer?" they asked. "Why, all day long, and all night long too, I sang," she replied. "Oh, you sang, did you?" said the ants. "Well, then, now you can dance."
Moral: Do not expect others to do the work you should have done.

36. The Traveller and his Dog

A traveller, about to set out on a journey, saw his dog stretching and yawning by the door. "What are you doing?" he said sharply. "Everything is ready but you, so come along quickly." The dog replied, "I have been waiting for you and am quite ready."
Moral: Don't accuse others of delaying you, when it is you who has been taking a long time.

THE · WILD · BOAR AND THE · FOX.

THE·CAT AND THE·MICE.

37. The Fox without a Tail

A fox who was once caught in a trap, was only able to get away by leaving his tail behind him. Afterwards he was very upset by the loss of his tail, but decided to make the best of it. He called together a meeting of all the other foxes to tell them how much better off he was without a tail, how free he felt and how much easier it was to run and jump, and he had almost persuaded the other foxes to be like him and all to cut off their tails. However, one old fox came forward and asked him if it was really for the benefit of the other foxes that he wished them to cut off their tails, or merely because it would help to disguise his own deformity.

Moral: Many people with serious defects try to get others to be like them.

38. The Cat and the Mice

A number of mice were peeping out of their hole to see if anyone was around when they saw a cat lying on a shelf. She looked so quiet and gentle that one of the mice said, "Well, I'll bet she's a good natured animal; you can see it in her face. I think I will go and make friends with her." So the mouse went up to her to do just that but, of course, as soon as the cat had the mouse within reach, she caught and ate him.

Moral: The look of something can mislead, and the look on a face not always reflect the mind.

39. The Hare and the Tortoise

"What a dull and slow animal is the tortoise", said a hare. The tortoise heard him and said, "I'll run a race with you for a bet." The hare agreed and they asked a fox to judge the contest. They started off together but the hare was soon so far ahead of the tortoise, who was just plodding along, that he decided to have a rest. He thought that he could easily overtake the tortoise at any time, but unfortunately he slept for too long and when he woke up, although he ran as fast as he could, he was amazed to find that the tortoise had plodded along without a break and reached the winning post before him. The tortoise had won the race.

Moral: If you make your way slowly but steadily you will get there in the end, but if you keep stopping and starting you may not get there at all.

40. The Gnat and the Bull

A bull was once driven by the heat of the weather to wade up to his knees in a cool stream. He had not been there long when a gnat flew upon one of his horns. "My dear fellow," said the gnat, buzzing very loudly, "please excuse me. If I am too heavy, just say so, and I will go at once and rest upon a tree growing by the stream." "It doesn't matter to me," replied the bull. "Had it not been for your buzz I should not even have known you were there."

Moral: Do not think yourself more important than you are.

THE·HARE AND THE·TORTOISE·

THE·LION AND THE·FOUR·BULLS.

41. The Hunter, the Fox and the Tiger

A hunter saw a fox in a field who had such a beautiful skin that he decided to catch him alive. With this in mind, he set a trap for the fox by digging a hole, covering it with twigs and straw, and putting some raw meat in it to attract the fox. He then went and hid to await the fox. The fox came and, smelling the meat, he went up to the pit but sensed that it was some trick and so did not jump in. A short while later a hungry tiger came and also smelled the meat. He sprang towards it and fell into the pit. Hearing the noise, the hunter ran up and thought the fox had fallen into his trap and without looking, he jumped in after him. He was amazed to find the tiger, who promptly ate him up.

Moral: If you set traps be careful not to be caught by your own cleverness.

42. The Lion and the Four Bulls

A group of four bulls formed a partnership to stay and feed together and to remain with each other in case of attack by any enemy. If a lion had met one of them alone he could easily have killed him but as long as they all four stayed together, they were safe. However, the bulls eventually began to quarrel amongst themselves and separated. The lion soon took advantage of this and easily hunted each down.

Moral: There is strength and safety in numbers and in staying together.

43. The Hare and the Hound

A dog was once chasing a fine hare, that proved himself to be a splendid runner. Eventually the dog, being out of breath, decided to give up the chase. The dog's owner teased him about giving up so easily and allowing himself to be beaten by a hare. "You don't understand," explained the dog. "He was running for his life, while I was only running for my dinner."
Moral: The circumstances you find yourself in will spur your actions.

44. The Kid and the Wolf

As a wolf was passing by a poor country cottage, a kid standing on the roof saw him and began shouting down all sorts of abuse. The wolf looked up and said, "If I had you down here on the ground, I would make you speak more politely".
Moral: A coward in a safe place makes a good deal more noise than the brave person in danger.

45. The Peacock and the Crane

As a peacock and a crane were walking together, the peacock spread out his beautiful tail and challenged the crane to show him as lovely a show of feathers. On hearing this the crane immediately flew up into the air and called to the peacock to follow him if he could. "You boast of your lovely plumes, which do certainly look wonderful, but they are of no use to you at all."
Moral: Nature gives useful and beautiful things, but the useful gifts are preferable to those of beauty alone.

THE·KID AND THE·WOLF.

THE·HARES AND·FROGS·

46. The Hares and the Frogs

Once upon a time all the hares were very unhappy because they thought that all the other creatures were trying to catch them and kill them. They were so tired of always having to run away from their enemies that they decided the only way out of their miserable lives was to kill themselves. Having decided this they all ran to the river to jump in and drown, but when they reached the river all the frogs who lived there ran away from them in fear. This made the hares think that maybe they were not so badly off after all and they decided to carry on living.

Moral: We can always find others worse off than ourselves.

47. The Wolf and the Fox

A very large and strong wolf was born among the wolves, much bigger, stronger and faster than all his fellow-wolves so that they gave him the nickname of "Lion". The wolf was foolish enough to believe that they had given him this name in earnest and left his own kind to go and live with the lions. An old fox said to him, "I hope I will never make myself as ridiculous as you with your pride and conceit. Here among the wolves you are like a lion, but once among the lions you will be no more than a wolf."

Moral: Do not deceive yourself into thinking you are something you are not.

48. The Covetous Man

A miser once buried all his money in the earth, at the foot of a tree, and went every day to gaze at the spot. A man who had seen him bury the treasure, came one night and stole it all. The next day the miser, finding a hole where his money had been, began to cry and scream with rage. One of his neighbours told him that if he looked at things differently, he would feel much better. "Cover the hole but go every day," he said, "and pretend your money is still there, and you will be as well off as ever."

Moral: There is point in owning something if you do not make use of it.

49. The Man and his Goose

A man owned a goose that laid golden eggs, which the man thought must come from a hidden mine inside the goose. He decided to cut her up and find this golden treasure, but when he did so, he found her to be just like other geese. The hope of getting more gold had lost him the source of what he already had.

Moral: If you love money too much and are not content with what you have, the desire to gain more may lose you everything.

THE ✦ MAN AND HIS GOOSE. ✿ ✿

THE·LEOPARD AND THE·FOX.

50. The Boy and the Hazlenut

A boy once put his hand into a jar which was full of figs and hazelnuts. He grasped as many as his fist could possibly hold but when he tried to draw his hand out, the narrowness of the neck prevented him. Not wanting to lose any but unable to take out his hand, he burst into tears.

Moral: Our own greed can prevent us from getting anything at all.

51. The Boasting Traveller

A man was once talking to a crowd of people and telling them of all the wonderful things he had done when on his travels. "I was once at Rhodes," he said, "where the people are famous for jumping. Well, I took a jump there that no other man could beat. It's quite true, and if I were there I could bring you ten men who could prove it." "What need is there to go to Rhodes for witnesses?" said one of the men listening, "just imagine you are there and show us your wonderful jump."

Moral: Do not boast about things that you cannot prove you can do, for you will be found out.

52. The Leopard and the Fox

A leopard was admiring the glossiness of his spotted skin, when a fox passing by whispered to him that the beauty of the mind was preferable to the beauty of a painted outside.

Moral: An understanding mind is better than all obvious beauties of the body.

53. The Boy and the Nettle

A little boy playing in the fields was stung by a nettle and came crying to his father. He told him he had been hurt by the nasty nettle before, and even though he had touched it ever so gently, the nettle had stung him so fiercely. His father said, "By touching it so gently and timidly, you made it sting all the more. A nettle needs to be handled with strength and if you will grasp it firmly, it will never sting you. The same is true of many people and things in this world which have to be treated in a similar manner."

Moral: Whatever you do, do it with strength of purpose and the courage of your convictions.

54. The Hawk and the Nightingale

As a nightingale was singing in a bush, down flew a hawk and caught her. The poor bird pleaded for her life, saying her little body was not worth eating and that there were much bigger birds to be found. "Well," said the hawk, "do you think I'd be stupid enough to let go of a little bird I have for a big one that I have not?" "All right," said the nightingale, "I will sing for you if you will spare my life." "No," said the hawk, "I want to eat you, not listen to you."

Moral: A bird in the hand is worth two in the bush.

THE·HAWK AND·THE NIGHTINGALE·

THE·PORCUPINE AND THE·SNAKES.

55. The Porcupine and the Snakes

One cold winter some snakes were persuaded to take a porcupine into their nest. When the porcupine was there, however, it was very narrow and his prickles were annoying to his companions so the snakes told him to look for somewhere else, as their place was too small for them all. "Well, then," said the porcupine, "he that cannot stay here should go, but personally I am quite happy where I am and if you are not, then you are perfectly free to move."
Moral: Once someone has possession of something, it is very difficult to make them let it go.

56. The Two Frogs

One hot summer, the lake in which two frogs lived was completely dried up, and they had to look somewhere else for water. They came to a deep, cool well and one of the frogs said that they should jump in at once. "Wait a bit," cried the other frog, "if this well should dry up, how could we get out again?"
Moral: Think of the possible result before taking precipitate action.

57. The Bear and the Bee-hives

A bear was once so angry at being stung by a bee that he rushed into the bee-garden and over-turned all the hives in revenge. This destruction brought all the bees out, who then attacked him and stung him a thousand times.
Moral: It is better to overlook one injury than to cause yourself to become the subject of many more.

58. The Dog and the Crocodile

A dog, running along the banks of a river, grew thirsty but afraid of being seized by a crocodile in the river, he did not stop to drink, but lapped at the water as he ran. The crocodile raised his head above the surface of the water and asked him why he was in such a hurry. He had often wished to make his acquaintance and now seemed like a good opportunity, the crocodile continued. "You do me a great honour," said the dog, "but it is to avoid such companions as you that I am in such a hurry."

Moral: It is best to know who your enemies are.

59. The Fox and the Grapes

Once upon a time a fox saw a lovely bunch of grapes hanging from a vine. He wanted them so much that he stood under the vine staring at them hungrily. He tried as hard as he could to reach them by jumping up and snatching at them, but he could not get near enough to eat any. At last he was very hot and tired and realised he could never reach them so he walked away disconsolately saying "Oh, well, I expect they were sour anyway".

Moral: When you know you cannot do something it will not help you to be too unhappy or disappointed. It is best to make light of it and pretend not to be disappointed.

THE·FOX AND THE·GRAPES.

THE·ASS·EATING·THISTLES.

60. The Ass Eating Thistles

There was once an ass who was trudging along, laden down with cakes and wine, chickens and all sorts of other good foods for his master and workmen to eat, when he saw a large, thick thistle and immediately started to eat it with a hearty appetite. "I bet," he thought to himself, "that if those men could see me now they would fall about laughing at the sight of this strange food. But this thistle, which tastes so good, is to me worth twenty of their fancy dishes."

Moral: One man's meat is another's poison.

61. The Lion and the Hare

A lion came across a hare who was fast asleep. He was just about to kill her when a young deer ran past and he decided to chase the deer instead. The hare was awoken by the noise and ran away. Meanwhile the lion chased the deer but could not catch her and decided to go back for the hare. When he found that the hare had also run away he said, "It serves me right for not taking the food I had in front of me for the chance of getting more."

Moral: Do not pass by something you are sure of for something of which you are uncertain.

62. The Ox and the Frog

A very large ox was grazing in a field and a frog was staring at him, very anxious because of his great size. The frog said to her children, "Look at that huge ox. See if I cannot make myself as big as he is". The frog began to swell and swell until she could get no bigger and eventually burst.

Moral: It is no good to try and become something you are not.

63. The Raven and the Swan

A raven decided that he would like to be as white as a swan and thought that the swan's whiteness must be due to all the time the swan spent in the water and the kind of food the swan ate. The raven then settled down to live in a lake, but of course being in water did not make his feathers white at all, and because he was not flying around he could not catch the food he usually ate and eventually starved to death.

Moral: You cannot change your basic nature and become something that you are not meant to be.

64. The Lioness and the Fox

A fox once remarked to a lioness that foxes were to be envied for having so many young ones. She said that every year she had a number of fox-cubs while some animals, she continued, had only one young one at a time and then not more than a few times in their lives. The lioness could not overlook this rudeness, and replied, "What you say is true; you have many cubs at a time but they all grow up to be foxes. I have but one, but that one is a lion."

Moral: Quality is more important than quantity.

THE·OX AND THE·FROG.

THE·WOLF AND THE·LION.

65. The Blind Man and the Lame Man

A blind man, trying to walk along a difficult road, met a lame man and asked him to guide him along the way. "I cannot do that," the lame man said, "as I can hardly walk, but if you could carry me we could go on together and I would show you the way, while you could be my feet." "Agreed," said the blind man, "it will be of mutual benefit for us to journey together." So they happily continued on their journey.

Moral: If you can help someone to overcome a difficulty, they can often be of help to you.

66. The Wolf and the Lion

There was once a wolf who stole a sheep and made off with it to his den. On his way he happened to meet a lion going hunting who, to his amazement, took hold of the sheep's body and went away with it. "Why, what's this?", called out the wolf, losing his temper, "Where is your conscience, that you steal from honest people?" The lion laughed at him and replied, "Would you have me believe that the shepherd gave you this sheep?"

Moral: Do not seek the protection of the law when you have already broken it yourself.

67. The Swan and the Goose

A man bought for himself a goose and a swan. He intended to fatten up the goose in order to eat him but to keep the swan for the sake of his singing. When the time came for killing the goose, his cook went to fetch the bird but it was dark and by mistake she took hold of the swan instead. The swan realized his danger and immediately began to sing so that he was recognized and released.

Moral: There comes a time when you must speak up for yourself.

68. The Fox and the Hare to Jupiter

A fox and a hare went to Jupiter to ask him if he would let the fox run as fast as the hare and the hare to be as clever as the fox. Jupiter told them that every creature has his own qualities and he could not give all the good qualities to every creature.

Moral: Everybody has his own special points and it would not be good if we all had the same ones.

69. The Bat and the Weasels

A bat fell to the ground and was caught by a weasel. The bat pleaded for his life but the weasel said he was the enemy of all birds. The bat then said he was not a bird, but a mouse, and the weasel let him go. Some time later he was caught by another weasel who said he hated all mice and was going to kill him. This time he said he was not a mouse, but a bird, and again he was released.

Moral: Turn all circumstances to your own good when in danger.

THE·FOX AND THE·HARE TO·JUPITER·

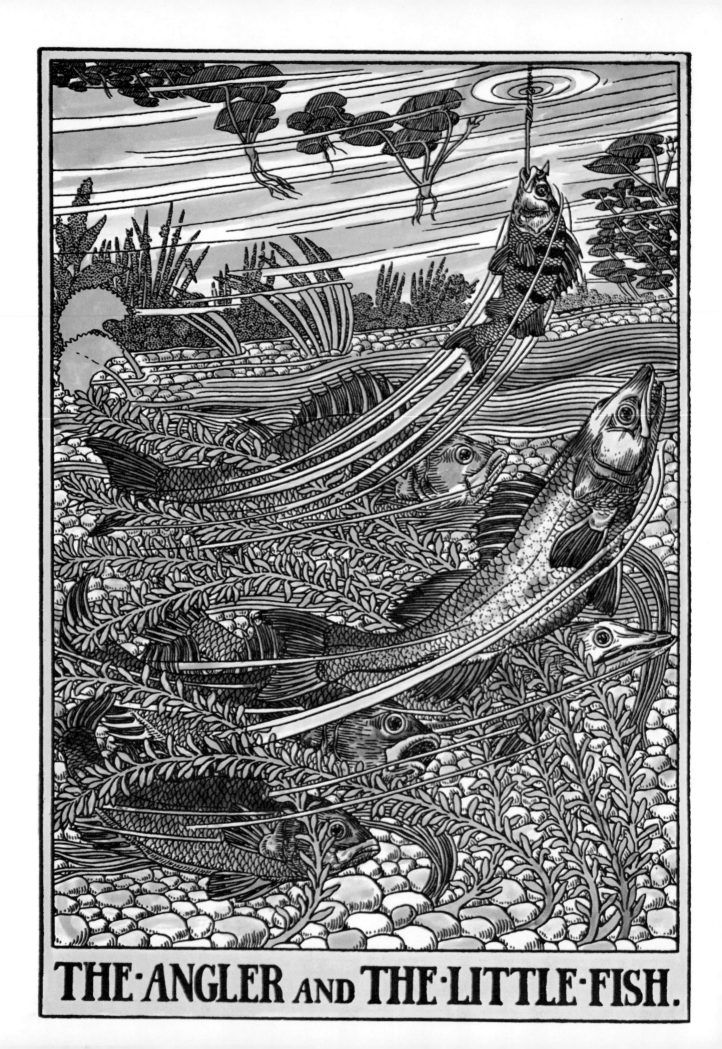

THE·ANGLER AND THE·LITTLE·FISH.

70. The Angler and the Little Fish

As an angler was fishing one day he happened to catch a very little fish. The tiny fish begged to be thrown back in the water and said, "I am not yet fully grown and if you will wait until I am bigger then you will have a much better catch." "Oh, no!", said the angler, "I would rather have you now, small as you are, than the promise of a bigger fish in the future."

Moral: It is best to take what we can while we have the opportunity than speculate for what may—or may not—happen.

71. The Spider and the Silkworm

A spider who was busy spreading his web from one side of the room to the other was asked by a silkworm why he spent so much time and effort in making so many lines and circles. The spider replied angrily, "Do not disturb me, you ignorant thing. I am leaving my skill for those after me and fame is what I am seeking." Just then, the lady of the house came into the room to feed her silkworms and saw the spider. With one stroke of her broom she swept both him and his web away.

Moral: Do not be too proud of your own achievements.

72. The Cat and the Fox

There was a debate between a fox and a cat as to which of the two could make the best of it if times became difficult. "For my part," said the fox, "when the worst comes to the worst, I have a whole bag of smart tricks to turn to." At that moment a pack of hunting dogs came towards them, barking loudly. The cat immediately climbed a tree and watched while the fox was torn to pieces. "Well," she said to herself, "my one sure trick is better than a hundred uncertain ones."

Moral: Nature provides us with our own means of survival better than we can ourselves.

73. The Hawk and the Farmer

A farmer happened to catch a hawk who was chasing a pigeon. The hawk pleaded to be set free, saying she had never done the farmer any harm, and hoping the farmer would do none to her. "Well," said the farmer, "and what harm was the pigeon doing to you? You must now expect to be treated as you would have treated the pigeon".

Moral: Think before you speak in case you condemn yourself with what you say.

THE·HAWK AND THE·FARMER.

THE·LION AND THE·MOUSE.

74. The Lion and the Mouse

A mouse heard a great moaning noise and came out to see what it was. She found it was a lion caught in a net. This reminded the mouse of how she had nearly been trodden on by a lion some time before, but the lion had kindly lifted his paw just in time. She discovered that this was the very same lion and so she set to work to nibble and gnaw away the ropes that were tying the lion, and eventually she managed to set him free.

Moral: It is good to help and be kind to each other, however great the differences between us.

75. The Lion, the Asses and the Hares

A war broke out between the birds and the animals, and the lion summoned all his subjects between the ages of sixteen and sixty to come before him dressed for battle. A number of hares and asses made their appearance. Several of his commanders wanted to turn them away as being totally unfit for service. "Do not be too hasty," said the lion, "the asses will do very well for trumpeters, and the hares will make excellent messengers."

Moral: Everybody has his own special uses.